Your C

Your Cross is Your Gift

Frank Bice

Frank Bice

Copyright © 2011 Frank Bice

ISBN 978-1-60910-744-4

All rights reserved. No part of this publication may be reproduced, stored in a retrieval system, or transmitted in any form or by any means, electronic, mechanical, recording or otherwise, without the prior written permission of the author.

Printed in the United States of America.

Bice & Bice, LLC
2011

First Edition

Bice & Bice, LLC
Manhasset, NY
www.frankbice.com

Your Cross is Your Gift

This book is dedicated to the little blond-haired girl who stole my heart on the first day of fourth grade.

Frank Bice

Your Cross is Your Gift

Table of Contents

Chapter I: Yes 1

Chapter II: Thank You, Jesus 7

Chapter III: Witnesses of Hope 13

Chapter IV: My Son, Your Sins Are Forgiven 21

Chapter V: Trust Me 29

Chapter VI: The Mustard Seed 37

Chapter VII: Come and Follow Me 43

Chapter VIII: The Exodus 51

Chapter IX: Do You Love Me? 65

Chapter X: The Resurrection 71

Frank Bice

Chapter I

Yes

In the fall of 1980, I was a senior at Siena College in Loudonville, New York. I was twenty-one years old and I was captain of my college football and lacrosse teams. As a safety in football, it was my job to prevent the other team from completing long passes against us. It was the third game of the season and I was having a pretty good year. I had three interceptions in the first two games and in that third game I picked off a pass in the first quarter. We were playing against St. John Fisher College in Rochester, New York. They had a great quarterback. This kid had a cannon for an arm. On this play, it was St. John Fisher's ball and it was a passing situation. They kept on splitting two receivers wide to one side of the field and we were in zone coverage. I was deep over the center of the field covering one of the receivers, when the quarterback threw a short pass to the tight end, who caught the ball and started running for a touchdown. In an effort to make a saving tackle, I came up and hit the receiver as hard as I could. The mistake I made was that I didn't get my head up in time and when our bodies collided, I broke my neck. As I lay on my back on the grass, all I knew was that I couldn't move or feel anything. When the trainers and coaches came out onto the field, they saw that I had a serious injury and called an ambulance. A student trainer named Jo-Ann knelt by my side and kept on reassuring me by saying, "It's OK, Frank. You're going to be OK." When the ambulance arrived they were able to put a board underneath my body and lift me into the vehicle.

St. John Fisher is a Catholic College and there was a priest at the game who got into the ambulance with me. On the way to the hospital, I was practically shouting Hail Marys over and over again. When I was a kid, my mother, brother, sisters, and I prayed the Rosary together as a family during the months of May and October. We would literally kneel in front of a statue of the Blessed Mother in our home and pray the Rosary. On the way to the emergency room, I desperately held onto that seed of faith that I had received as a kid. I was scared to death. Praying Hail Marys in the ambulance and having the priest with me was a huge consolation.

Once inside the hospital, the doctors and nurses unscrewed my facemask, cut off my jersey and shoulder pads, and took a series of x-rays. They explained that I had broken my neck, I'd never walk again, and that they weren't sure if I was going to live. The priest gave me the Anointing of the Sick and then heard my confession right in front of all the doctors and nurses. My confession lasted a good five minutes. I thought that if I was going to die, I was going with a clean slate!

The nurses then shaved my head and a doctor approached me with a Black & Decker drill in his hand. The physician said, "I'm sorry, but we need to stabilize your head and neck. Your injury is too close to your brain for sedation." While the nurses held my head steady, the doctor proceeded to drill six screws into my scull to apply a metal brace called a "halo." I'd like to tell you that I bit the bullet and took it like a man. I didn't. The pain was excruciating. I screamed and cried until I passed out from the pain.

When I woke up two hours later, I was in traction. They secured my body on a Stryker fame. This was a narrow bed that was suspended between two points, (the bed almost looked like a hammock that you might see in someone's backyard, suspended in the air and supported at either end). During this time they kept my head, neck, and lower extremities completely straight and immobilized. A few days after my injury, they surgically removed a piece of bone from my hip and used it to fuse the fifth and sixth cervical vertebrae in my spine.

I spent the next month in traction. To ensure proper circulation and to relieve pressure from building up on any one part of my body, I'd face the ceiling for two hours and then they would strap my body to the frame and flip it over so I could face the floor for two hours. They rotated my body every two hours for a month.

During this time, my family and friends were incredibly supportive. My buddies were really funny. Like most college kids, my teammates and I took pride in shattering social boundaries. My area in the hospital turned into a locker room. I had friends sleeping on the floor and hiding in closets and bathrooms after visiting hours. Some would wear hospital gowns and ride around the halls in wheelchairs so that the staff would believe that they were newly injured patients.

One of my buddies used to write notes to the nurses on my body with a magic marker. A high school friend brought in a fake hand that looked real and hid it under my sheet. When the nurse rotated my Stryker frame, the fake hand fell on the floor and the nurse screamed and ran out of the room!

In the middle of the night, when my friends weren't around, I had time to pray. One night, while I was praying, I made a deal with God. My prayer went something like this: "Lord, I know my life has not been perfect. I know no one's life is perfect. Even if I didn't have this injury, my life was never going to be perfect anyway. If You will give me grace to live the rest of my life with a positive attitude, I will say, 'Yes,' to whatever You ask me to do." In other words, I surrendered.

When I finally got out of traction, and was able to sit in a wheelchair for a short amount of time, a nurse came in my room and asked me to visit a newly injured patient down the hall. Believe me, the last thing I wanted to do was to visit another newly injured patient. I said, "Yes," because that was the deal I had made with God. After I visited with the young man, as the nurse wheeled me back to my room, I couldn't believe how good I felt. I realized that saying, "Yes," would lead to new possibilities and situations, and more often than not, would lead to some type of service. I learned early on that any type of service would set you free.

Chapter II
Thank You, Jesus

After receiving excellent medical care at Strong Memorial Hospital in Rochester, I was flown by an air ambulance to a major rehabilitation hospital in New York City called the Rusk Institute.

At Rusk, I was placed in a room with three other patients. There was Jacob, a newly injured, seventeen year old quadriplegic, who had become disabled as a result of a diving accident. Jacob had been working as a lifeguard the previous summer. To impress a young lady, he dove off the lifeguard stand, hit the bottom of the pool, and became completely paralyzed from the neck down. As a result of his high level injury, Jacob didn't have any arm movement. Jacob was extremely bright, but sometimes his frustration would get the better of him. During these times he would scream and curse at the nurses and aids. This was New York

City and the staff was very tough. When the aids had enough of Jacob's verbal abuse, they would take his paralyzed thumb and hold it in his mouth and ask, "Does the baby want to suck his thumb?" This would drive Jacob to the brink of insanity. When Jacob was especially vicious in his verbal assault, a nurse would press her nose up against his cheek and ask, "If you hate me so much, why don't you hit me?" This would cause Jacob to explode.

My other two roommates were Mike and Seamus. These guys were the same age as me and we also shared the same level of injury. The three of us were C5-6 quadriplegics, which meant that we were completely paralyzed from the chest down, and we had partial paralysis in our arms and hands. Mike had been in Trenton State Prison for attempted manslaughter, got out, dove off a bridge into a river, hit a sandbar, and broke his neck. Seamus had been in Rikers Island Prison for stealing cars, got out, dove off the roof of his friend's house into a pool, hit the bottom, and became a quadriplegic.

If you had to be in the hospital, these were the guys you'd want to be with. There was never a dull moment! Mike was especially crazy. Every morning, the nurses would spend about an hour preparing the medicine cart with the pills to be distributed among the patients in our wing of the hospital. Almost every morning, Mike would flip over the medicine cart and the pills would fly down the hallway. The nurses wanted to kill him! In order to eat our meals, we would be seated in our wheelchairs and they would place trays of food on small tables that could swing over our laps. If Mike was unhappy with our dining selection, he would toss the tray over his head and we would all have to take cover as the plates and silverware went flying. Because of the lack of grip in our hands, they secured our knives and forks in holders, called "C Clips," that fit on our hands. The problem with this method was Mike's inability to control his temper. During mealtime, if anyone came into our room and got on Mike's nerves, those utensils quickly turned into weapons. With the agility of a black belt in karate, Mike would stab people, literally. If Mike was in a really bad mood, he would bite people. Every now and then an unsuspecting visitor would be caught off guard, and Mike would clamp his teeth upon his victim's arm or leg and they would scream for help. So you really had to watch yourself around Mike. Thank God he liked me.

Our other roommate, Seamus, suffered from a good case of Irish guilt. He genuinely regretted the heartache that his trouble-filled days as a youth had caused his family. Seamus was a big sports fan. He loved the Mets. He had a great group of loyal friends who used to visit him from Queens. Their nickname for him was "Goat." I didn't want to know how they came up with that nickname. Seamus was really a great kid.

While I was a patient at Rusk, a very significant thing started happening that changed my life. Every now and then, a priest from St. Mary's in Manhasset used to come and visit me. I didn't know this priest before my injury, but when he would come to see me, he would pray in my ear, "Thank You, Jesus," over and over again. That simple prayer, "Thank You, Jesus," changed my life. At first I thought that it was a little strange that this priest would pray that prayer in my ear over and over again, but honestly, it was the greatest gift he could have given me. After he would leave the hospital, I would find myself praying, "Thank You, Jesus, Thank You, Jesus, Thank You, Jesus," over and over again. I would pray that prayer when I first woke up in the morning. I would pray, "Thank You, Jesus," during physical therapy classes. I would pray it all day long. I would pray, "Thank You, Jesus," as I went to sleep at night.

I came to understand that this simple prayer is the secret to life. As I would pray, "Thank You, Jesus," over and over again, I began to understand how much I had to be grateful for in my life. I became grateful for my wonderful family, my great friends, the excellent nurses and therapists, the hospital, and my good health. Even though I had a serious injury, I realized that my body was still strong and that I had a bright future. I became so optimistic that the doctors and nurses started to believe that I was crazy. I became grateful for everything. I even became grateful for my injury, if you can believe it. As I prayed that prayer, "Thank You, Jesus," I came to understand that my Cross was my Gift. I realized that my injury would give me a whole new perspective on life. The outpouring of love I received from my family and friends was incredible. I realized that my job was easy. All I had to do was say, "Yes," anytime anybody asked me to do anything, (as long as it was a good thing), and God would give me the grace to have a positive attitude. And now the prayer, "Thank You, Jesus," totally set me free. Even the slightest hint of any frustration or depression associated with my injury was completely gone forever. Now, I don't mean to say that my life would become completely trouble free and without challenges or heartaches. What I'm saying is that any regret or wistful reminiscing about the good old days or the way things might been were lifted by the prayer, "Thank You, Jesus." That simple prayer takes control of your heart, mind, and soul and always produces a positive outcome. It creates an overwhelming sense of gratitude which is the foundation of faith because you expect something good to happen and then something good always happens. This is not wishful thinking; it is a fact of life.

Chapter III
Witnesses of Hope

While I was in the hospital, we would have different therapy classes during the day. At nights and on weekends, they had a school bus that would transport us to Madison Square Garden for Knick games or boxing matches. One weekend, they advertised a trip to a wheelchair sports meet. Seamus, Mike, and I decided to go. While we were there, a coach from the New Jersey Wheelers approached me and asked if I would join their team. I said, "Yes."

The next weekend I found myself in the middle of a football stadium at a major university with a shot put in my hand. I had joined the New Jersey Wheelers and I was competing against the national champ. The shot put is like a small metal bowling ball. It feels like it weighs a ton! At the competition, when I threw the shot put, it barely cleared my chair. It almost fell on my lap and I thought, "Wow, that would have hurt!" The national champ threw his shot put about thirty feet. I think he set a world record. The next event called for us to throw the disk. The disk is like a small metal Frisbee. It should float through the air like a Frisbee. When I threw the disk, it strained end over end and flopped on the grass. It traveled about four feet. The national champ threw his disk about fifty feet. I think he set another world record. The final event was the club throw. The club is a small, wooden bowling pin. It's designed for guys to throw who have paralysis in their hands. I threw the club about five feet. The national champ threw his club practically out of the stadium. I got crushed in every event.

The following day I was signed up for the fifty yard dash. I was on the starting line, next to all of these other guys in wheelchairs when "Bang" the gun went off! A fifty-yard race in a wheelchair should take only seconds to complete. When I went to push my chair, it didn't move. One of my front wheels was jammed, but eventually I started to be able to creep along. It was taking me minutes to get down the track. My coach was even walking next to me saying, "Frank, please, you don't have to finish, they want to start the next event." I said, "Coach, I started this race; I have to finish it!" As I was lumbering down the track, I noticed that one of the guys I was racing against had fallen out of his chair and was unconscious on the ground. As I went by him, at first I felt really bad. Then I thought, "At least I might not come in last!" Well, believe it or not, they revived him, got him back in his chair, and he beat me at the finish line. It served me right for not having very much compassion for my fellow wheelchair athlete. After that race, I was proud of myself for finishing, but a little embarrassed that it took me over eight minutes to go fifty yards. That weekend I learned that saying, "Yes," would lead to new possibilities and experiences, and, it was fun to get out there and to compete again.

During my stay in the hospital, I became friends with a twenty-seven year old patient down the hall named Vin. Vinny had been a teacher at Holy Family High School in Huntington, New York. He was newly married to a beautiful woman named Ann. One day while Vinny was teaching in class, he got dizzy and fainted. In the emergency room, he slipped into a coma. When Vin woke up, after being unconscious for several weeks, he was paralyzed. The doctors believed that he had been bitten by an insect, had an allergic reaction which infected his central nervous system, and he became a quadriplegic.

While Vinny was in the hospital, he was almost always too sick to get out of bed. He suffered from pressure sores, kidney infections, and pneumonia. When I would visit with Vinny, he was always upbeat and positive. Vin's wife, Ann, would visit in the evenings. Like Vinny, Ann was always so hopeful and enthusiastic about their future. When it was time for Vin to go home, he had been in the hospital for eighteen months. This is Vinny and Ann's story.

Ann purchased a hospital bed and set it in their living room. An ambulance brought Vin home from the hospital and he was placed in that bed, where he remained for years.

When I first got out of the hospital, a buddy and I rode out to see Vinny and Ann. We visited with Vin from his bedside. As usual, Vin was very cheerful. Then years went by, and I fell out of touch with Vinny. I had wanted to call, but I was afraid because I thought that Vin might have passed away. One day, I finally got up the nerve to call Vinny. Ann answered the phone and she sounded great. She held the phone for Vinny and he sounded the same as when we were in the hospital together: upbeat and positive. As we were speaking, I heard a lot of noise in the background. When I asked Vin about all of the racket in his house, he told me that he and Ann had adopted three boys. Vin explained that Ann was an awesome mom, and that even though he was still in bed, he could help the boys with their homework and other activities. When I hung up the phone, I couldn't believe it. This man couldn't even get out of bed, and he and his beautiful wife, Ann, had the courage to adopt three boys.

A few more years passed and I called Vinny and Ann again. Now it sounded like World War III in the background. I asked Vin, "What is all that noise?" He explained that they had adopted three more boys. They had adopted six boys! And three of the boys were named Joseph! So they had Joseph, Joey, and Joe. I couldn't believe it. Vinny and Ann didn't let anything stop them from fulfilling their dream.

In his Encyclical on the Eucharist, Pope John Paul II calls all Catholics to be Witnesses of Hope. Vin and Ann truly were Witnesses of Hope because they embraced their Cross and went ahead with their lives despite incredible physical, emotional, spiritual, and financial challenges. At Sunday Mass each week, Ann would be seen in church with all six boys wearing shirts and ties. Ann and Vin impressed upon their sons the value of sharing in the Eucharist, which in Greek means "Thanksgiving." By their example, Ann and Vinny, taught the boys to live lives of gratitude; to be Witnesses of Hope.

At the Last Supper, when Jesus instituted the Eucharist by saying, "Do this in memory of Me," He extended an invitation to the human race to live their lives in a new context. By participating in this Sacred Meal, through the centuries Christians have entered into the mystery of dying to themselves and allowing Christ to live in them. As individuals, Christians understand that Christ not only lives in them, but in those with whom they share Communion. By embracing this concept, Vinny and Ann were able to live out their existence in heroic fashion. The love that was shared by Ann and Vinny transcended their own limitations and lit a fire. Where did Ann and Vin find the inspiration and the amazing courage to be able to lay down their lives for their sons? They found it in the Eucharist. The fire of their love now burns brightly in the hearts of their sons. Vinny and Ann, by entering into the death and resurrection of Jesus through their participation in the Eucharist, became Witnesses of Hope for their sons.

Frank Bice

Chapter IV
My Son, Your Sins Are Forgiven

After spending eight months in the hospital, my family had generously made our home wheelchair accessible. My first night back home I slept in a room downstairs. When I woke up, something horrifying happened. I opened my eyes and I was looking into the faces of two of the Miller brothers. If you are from Manhasset, you probably know the Millers. There are ten brothers and two sisters in this family and these guys are nuts!

So I said, "Oh, hey fellas, what's up?" They replied, "We're here to take you swimming." I asked, "Swimming? Have you guys noticed the wheelchair? I'm paralyzed. I can't go swimming!" They answered, "We don't care. Our Mom got you a waterskiing vest so that you can go swimming in our grandparents' pool. Let's go." The next thing I know, I have the vest on and I'm doing laps in their grandparents' pool. Every day that summer, two of the Millers showed up and took me swimming. Believe me, it was the last thing I wanted to do, but it was the best thing for me. By the end of the summer, I could actually swim a mile.

Every now and then, the Millers would take me to the beach. We would either go to Jones Beach or out to the Hamptons and they would carry me into the ocean. Once they guided me past where the waves were breaking, I could swim on my back. Now, I'll be honest with you, I was never that comfortable swimming in the ocean. I never really felt I was in control of the situation, but the salt water was great for my skin and it was good exercise.

One Saturday morning, we headed out to the Hamptons. The night before there had been a heavy storm. When we arrived at the beach, the red flags were blowing in the wind and the waves were huge. When the Miller brothers took out my waterskiing vest, I was about to say, "No," probably for the first time since my injury, but they looked at me and said, "You're going in." The next thing you know, I have the vest on and one of the guys has me in a bear hug and the other has me by the legs. As they carried me into the ocean, the waves were killing us. When we finally got passed where the waves were breaking, the swells got a hold of my body and I started going out to sea and down the coast. These were eight foot swells! I was afraid, and then something terrifying happened. When I was on the top of one of those waves, I saw Eugene Miller, from a distance, had a look of fear in his eyes. I had known this kid for my entire life. Not once had I seen any trace of fear in him at anytime. When he looked afraid, I became petrified.

The Gospel describes a situation where Jesus is teaching in a house that is standing room only. When a group of friends bring a paralyzed man to see Jesus, they can't get in because of the crowd. So they cut a hole in the roof and lower the paralyzed man right in front of Jesus. As the story goes, Jesus, seeing the faith of the friends of the paralyzed man, says, "My son, your sins are forgiven." Now when Jesus says this, He understands that He is going to get a reaction from the religious leaders who are present in the crowd. He knows that they are thinking, "Who is He to forgive sins? Can't only God forgive sins?" Sensing that they are angry with Him, Jesus says, "Which is easier to say, 'Your sins are forgiven' or 'Rise and walk!'" The paralyzed man immediately gets up and starts giving glory to God.

This story gives us a great insight into the mission of Jesus. The mission of Jesus involved preaching the Good News in an effort to repair our relationship with God and each other. If you look at the Old Testament, in the beginning, human beings live in perfect harmony with each other, their environment, and, most importantly, with God. After Adam and Eve sin, the remainder of the Hebrew Scriptures is dedicated to describing the ups and downs of our relationship with God and each other. After Noah and the flood, God gives us a second chance by establishing His covenant with Abraham. The one requirement that God asks of those whom He chooses is faithfulness. The salvation history of the Israelites begins to focus on the coming of the Anointed One, the Messiah. The Messiah was going to reunite the people of God, and as one nation they would lead all the other nations on the path toward God. That is why Jesus chose twelve Jewish men as his Apostles, to symbolize the unification of the twelve tribes of Israel that had become fragmented through the centuries. For His part as the Messiah, Jesus understood that His mission would entail surrendering to the will of His Father. In His faithfulness, which ultimately led to His crucifixion, Jesus completely reverses the lack of trust exhibited by Adam and Eve. That is why Jesus is referred to as the New Adam in the New Testament. The mission of Jesus was first, and foremost, about restoring that loving, trusting, and intimate relationship that human beings were meant to share with God as it is described in the Garden of Eden. Jesus even went so far as to encourage us to call God, Dad. Now, I don't know about you, but when I pray and I refer to God as Dad, it makes me feel really uncomfortable. Why did Jesus encourage us to call God, Dad? Because He wanted us to exist in the right, loving, relationship with our Father who loves us so much that He knows every hair on our head and every breath we take. He knows our every hope and desire. Jesus wanted us to understand that we have a Father who loves us unconditionally, who is crazy about us, and who is always there for us. The healings in the ministry of Jesus are always secondary to Jesus restoring that right relationship meant to exist between God and us. The healings are referred to as a "sign" that the Kingdom of Heaven is at hand. Nothing in our lives is as important as living in the right relationship with God our Father. The miracle and main reason to celebrate in the story of the paralyzed man in the Gospel was not because he was able to walk again. It was because Jesus forgave his sins! The man could begin a new life in the right relationship with God, his Father, and the community.

On that note, that day, when I was floating on the waves (scared to death) let's imagine that Jesus had appeared to me walking on the water. Let's imagine Jesus had said, "Frank, My son, your sins are forgiven." I think I probably would have said, "Oh Jesus, thank God you're here! And thank You so much for forgiving my sins. I know I have a lot of them. But, while You're at it, do you think You can help me get me back to the beach?" Now, the reason I say this is because I want my problems solved through the eyes of the world. If I really trust God to the point where I can see my Cross as my Gift, I can view my difficulties as an opportunity to pray for more faith. So often, Jesus encourages His disciples to, "Pray for more faith." When He does heal someone, He says, "It's your faith that healed you." In that light, in the face of difficulties or what may seem like impossible challenges, we can have the confident assurance that God will carry us through. Our job is easy. By our ability to remain optimistic, to stay positive and to really trust God, we can live in that right relationship that Jesus was talking about.

Finally that day, Eugene Miller swam out and got a hold of my foot and dragged me to shore and we were all OK. Before his courageous rescue, I wound up being a half-mile off the shore and another half-mile down the coast!

Frank Bice

Chapter V
Trust Me

The summer that I was first home from the hospital, I had to decide how I was going to finish my last year of college. I didn't want to go back to my old college because I thought that everyone would remember me the way I was before my injury, and now I would be going back in a wheelchair. Both my football and lacrosse coaches encouraged me to come back and said that I could serve as an assistant coach on each team. My friends and teammates encouraged me to come back. The deciding factor was my friend, Rence.

I'm about to describe how my buddy, Rence, helped me. As I describe this relationship, I do not in anyway mean to overlook or show a lack of appreciation for the amazing generosity of my family and many other friends. This chapter could have been dedicated to almost any member of my family and to numerous friends. To illustrate my message, and for reasons involving time and clarity, the character of Rence embodies the spirit of so many incredible people in my life.

When I was in high school, I went away to boarding school. As an eighth grader, I was reluctant to be away from home for high school. It turned out to be the best thing for me. One of my best friends was a really creative, generous, and funny kid named, Rence. Rence played football and was one of the top wrestlers in the school.

After high school graduation, Rence and I attended separate colleges. After a year and a half, Rence transferred to Siena. Before long, Rence took the college by storm. He started dating a beautiful girl named Virginia, played on the football team, and became the most popular kid on campus. Rence's charm, wit, humility, and incredible sense of humor, made him a legend on campus. Although when Rence transferred into Siena, he lost a lot of credits and wound up being a year behind me.

The day of my injury, Rence was on the football team. I can't describe what a huge consolation it was to have an old friend with me when I had my accident and during those first few days in the hospital. At the end of the following summer, it was time for me to decide what I should do about college. Rence said that if I came back to Siena he would be my roommate and that he would take care of everything. I said, "Yes."

When I went back for my second senior year in college, everyday for nine months, Rence got me up, helped me take a shower, got me dressed, helped me go to the bathroom, pushed me in my chair to class, wheeled me to football and lacrosse practices, and helped me go to bed at night. Rence, everyday for nine months, served so joyfully and made it so much fun, that we were laughing hysterically for the entire year. Anyone who witnessed the way Rence assisted me, couldn't help bursting into a fit of laughter.

That year, Rence and I took a Greek mythology class. An incredibly kind-hearted, brilliant, short, chubby, completely bald, ancient, Franciscan priest, named Father Liguori Mueller taught the course. Father Mueller, dressed in his brown, Franciscan robe, resembled an elderly and smaller version of the cartoon character, Shrek. We concluded that Father Mueller was an authority on Greek mythology because he must have been alive in antiquity, when polytheism was the rule of the day.

Father Mueller's nickname was "Mule Train." As Rence would push me into class, usually a few minutes late, he would pretend he was driving a stagecoach, whipping the imaginary horses in front of my wheelchair. Rence would sing the lyrics from "Rawhide," bellowing, "Rollin', rollin', rollin', keep them doggies rollin'..." At the end of several verses, Rence would conclude his song by substituting "Mule Train!" for "Rawhide!"

Father Mueller started his class with the dual ritual of leading us in a prayer and then lighting a non-filtered cigarette. He would sit there in his brown, Franciscan robe, chain-smoking for the entire eighty-minute class. Father would take a huge drag off of his cigarette, but you'd never see him exhale. We concluded that this must have been some sort of mendicant ritual and the secret behind Father's longevity.

Father Mueller would lecture for twenty minutes, and then he would call on us to read the stories from our textbooks. The class was painfully boring. To make things interesting, we would try to distract the student who had been called upon to read. When it was your turn, you had to do everything in your power to defend yourself. While you were reading, one of your classmates might reach over and slap you on the head or try to close your book. As the semester progressed, the onslaught from the thugs sitting around you became more intense. You might receive a shot to the ribs, a Charlie Horse inflicted upon your leg, or a page actually ripped out of your book. During the last class of the semester, I had been called upon to read, and my disability didn't preclude me from the friendly fire. As I was reading, Rence reached over and unlocked the brakes on my wheelchair. The gentleman sitting behind me put both feet on the back of my chair and pushed as hard as he could. I went flying to the front of the classroom and hit my head on the blackboard! In mid-drag of his cigarette, Father Mueller turned and asked, "What's the matter with you?" I replied, "I'm sorry Father, I just had a muscle spasm."

My second senior year in college was great in everyway possible. During spring break, fourteen of us rented a Winnebago, and headed down to Fort Lauderdale. I sat on a couch in the back of the vehicle and held on for dear life. The trip was a blast. All of my friends made me feel completely accepted and appreciated. I was included in everything and I never once felt like I was imposing in anyway.

At the Last Supper, when Jesus washed the feet of the disciples, He taught us that to be great in the Kingdom of Heaven, we have to serve. Jesus also said something in the Gospel that always confused me. When the disciples didn't want Him to leave them, Jesus assured them that if He went home to the Father, He would send His Spirit and His followers would do even greater works than He did. Now, even though Jesus said this, I never believed it. I mean, how could anyone ever do greater works than Jesus? Well if you witnessed the way Rence, literally, carried me through my second senior year at college, you would know that the words of Jesus were true.

When Rence served, he made it so much fun, that the person being served felt absolutely wonderful. I felt so great that entire year that, honestly, the year that I went back to college in a wheelchair was my best year in college. I loved it. That year, Rence set me free. His spirit and enthusiasm set the entire college free. Rence gives us an excellent example of how we should serve. We should see service as an honor and a privilege. We should never serve out of obligation. We should always strive to make service fun. If you know someone who is suffering and you don't know what to do, just show up. Just be there. When in doubt, just show up. Say "Yes" to service and make it fun.

Frank Bice

Chapter VI
The Mustard Seed

When I arrived back home after graduating from college, my friends had a fundraiser and bought me a van that I could drive with hand controls. Their generosity gave me an incredible amount of freedom. Almost immediately, I got into coaching. One of my first jobs was coaching the Boys' Junior Varsity Lacrosse Team at St. Mary's in Manhasset.

The routine was basically the same everyday. I would drive my van to the field, my players would meet me and push me in my chair to the field and we would have practice. The kids were great. My chair disappeared and we had an excellent season. Something started happening that year that I will never forget. Almost everyday, before I got out of my van, a kid named Dave would approach the driver's side window and say, "Coach, I made a big mistake. I'm playing baseball, but I know I should be playing lacrosse." Dave was a sixteen-year old sophomore at the time. Finally one day I said to him, "Dave, you seem like you're in a lot of pain. What's going on in your life?" Dave replied, "My parents are going through a divorce and it's killing me. My dad was a baseball star. I've been playing baseball to try and heal that relationship in my family, but I can't do it. I know I should be playing lacrosse." I explained to Dave that I would be coaching summer league lacrosse at Manhasset High School and that he should come out. He said, "Don't worry, Coach, I'm definitely coming out for summer league."

That summer Dave came out with a defenseman's stick and all of his equipment. He was a big kid, over six feet tall, a natural lefty, a good athlete, and very aggressive. After we played a few summer league games, Dave gave me a list of five Division I college coaches to whom he urged me to write letters. He wanted me to inform them that he needed a full scholarship for lacrosse. I tried to tell Dave that it was too soon to write the letters because he hadn't even played in a varsity game yet. Dave said, "Don't worry, Coach, I'm going to be awesome. Please just write the letters." So I tried to avoid Dave after that because I didn't want to write the letters. To his credit and because of his belief in himself, Dave wouldn't take "No" for an answer. Dave called my house everyday. Dave even showed up at my house asking if I had written the letters. Finally, just to get Dave off of my back, I wrote to the five college coaches. I only heard back from one coach who said it was still too early to take a look at Dave.

This is Dave's story. Dave took all of the heartache and pain in his life and he took a step back. In the midst of his parents' divorce, he realized that he had a unique gift that no one else realized he had. Dave took all of his frustration and channeled it into something incredibly positive: becoming the best lacrosse player he could possibly become. From that time on, you never saw Dave without his lacrosse stick in his hands. Everyday, Dave ran sprints, lifted weights, and worked harder than anyone else at becoming a great lacrosse player.

In Dave's junior year, he made varsity and earned a starting position. Before long, Dave really started to dominate. The next summer, Dave made the Long Island Empire State Team. This is an incredible lacrosse team comprised of high school All-Stars who play against other All-Star select teams from all over New York State. Dave continued to carry his lacrosse stick wherever he went. He also kept growing.

As a senior in high school, Dave was amazing. He made High School All-American and earned a full scholarship to Johns Hopkins University. At Hopkins, in Dave's freshman year he got sick and saw limited action. As a sophomore, Dave made 1st Team All-American and his team won the National Championship. In Dave's junior year, he made 1st Team All-American. As a senior, Dave made 1st Team All-American and was named Player of the Year in Division I College Lacrosse. Dave was named Player of the Year as a defenseman, which is almost impossible. That award usually goes to a really high scorer, an attackman or middy. Dave was named Player of the Year as a defenseman!

After college, Dave played on the United States Lacrosse Team. In the World Games in Australia, the United States defeated Canada, and Dave was named the Most Valuable Player of the World Games. So just a few years earlier, this kid Dave is walking up to my van everyday saying, "Coach, I'm playing baseball, but I know I should be playing lacrosse." Now he's named the greatest lacrosse player on the planet Earth!

When Jesus wanted people to understand His message, He taught in parables. A parable can be defined as a story with a double meaning. Jesus used parables as a teaching method because He comprehended human nature. Jesus understood that we need to come to terms with the truth by figuring it out for ourselves. One of the major themes that Jesus tried to express in His ministry was the mysteriousness of the Kingdom of Heaven. An element of the Kingdom of Heaven to which Jesus continually referred was the power of faith. To illustrate the power of faith, Jesus gave us the Parable of the Mustard Seed. Jesus said that when you hold a mustard seed in your hand, it is the smallest of seeds. No one would ever expect that a mighty tree could grow out of that tiny seed. Ultimately, the seed produces a tree in which the birds of the air can build their nests, we can be shaded from the sun, and we can be fed of its fruit. All from what seems like nothing!

I can't think of a better modern day parable that illustrates the mysteriousness of the Kingdom of Heaven and the power of faith than the life of the young man, Dave. Dave went from playing baseball as a sophomore in high school to being named the greatest lacrosse player in the world! Like the mustard seed, the power of Dave's faith expanded his talent and ability to unimaginable heights. Dave's ability to transcend and transform his heartache and pain into something so awesome stands as a monument to the power of determination and faith. The modern day parable of Dave's life challenges us all to question if we are living up to our potential. Dave's success also serves as a warning that we should never underestimate another person's ability.

Chapter VII
Come and Follow Me

During the early years after my injury, I began to go to Mass every morning before work. I took a job as a service representative with New York Telephone and continued to coach in the evenings and on weekends. A local newspaper, the *Long Island Catholic,* did a story on my coaching. Shortly after that article was printed, two young priests asked me to speak to the youth groups at their respective parishes. After I gave those talks, both priests asked me if I would consider the priesthood. Now the deal I had made with God was that I would say "Yes" to whatever I perceived to be His will. My problem was that I always wanted to get married. So I prayed about where God was calling me and I decided that if this was God's will, I better say "Yes."

One of the young priests made arrangements for me to meet with Bishop McGann, who was the head of the Diocese of Rockville Centre. Because of my disability, my situation was unique, and I needed permission from the Bishop to proceed with the application process. The Bishop advised me that there was an admission board in place and if they accepted me into the seminary, he would not stand in my way.

So I completed the entire admissions process without telling a soul. I was fairly certain that I was never going to be accepted anyway, and so no one would have to know about it. On my birthday, March 25, 1987, I received my acceptance letter. I couldn't believe it. I thought, "My God, what am I going to do?" I decided to say, "Yes."

When I was accepted to the seminary, they made one very reasonable stipulation. The stipulation was that, if, at anytime, I believed that I couldn't handle the responsibilities associated with the priesthood because of my disability, I would step down on my own. I agreed.

My years in the seminary were awesome. I completed a year of philosophy, two years of theology, and my pastoral year. I loved every minute of it. The classes were really challenging, but I loved them. The formation program included prayer (morning, evening, and night), daily mass, spiritual direction, and a very demanding course load. My fellow seminarians were the greatest guys in the world. The Bishop even allowed me to bring my golden retriever, named Jugger, to live with me. My dog's name was really, JUG, which stood for Justice Under God. JUG was the old Jesuit form of punishment and the name of a legendary golden retriever at my old boarding school. At the seminary, I was treated with the utmost respect, generosity, and kindness.

During my years in the seminary, my two best friends were Brian Barr and Jimmy Scacalossi. Brian, a graduate of Cornell, came from a great family. He loved playing Irish music on the banjo. Jimmy also came from a great family and was super bright. Jim graduated from Regis High School in New York City and earned his degree from St. John's University in three years. The problem with Jimmy was his uncanny ability to physically hurt anyone who came near him. The name Scacalossi means "Bone Breaker" in Italian. One day, while I was rolling into Church History Class, Jimmy went to slap me on the back of the head and hit my eye by accident. For the entire class my eye was watering like crazy. That same day after class, I was sitting in my room, waiting for Brian and Jimmy to get me for Mass. Jimmy burst in my room, picked up a towel and went to "rat tail" me. To "rat tail" someone is a technique employed by an individual whereby he rolls up a towel and basically whips his victim in order to inflict as much pain as possible. As Jimmy snapped the towel in the direction of my head, he hit my other eye. In one day, Jimmy almost blinded me.

Almost everyday, after class, Jimmy, Brian and I would take my dog, Jug, for a long run across the seminary property. One day while we were out for a walk, we stumbled across a cabin in the woods with a fireplace. We just looked at each other and said, "We know where we are coming tonight!" That night, and many nights after that, we headed out to the cabin with a bunch of seminarians. We would light a fire, smoke cigars, and drink a few beers while Brian played the banjo. Jug would position himself by the front door of the cabin and serve as guard dog. These were awesome nights.

After I had completed my year of philosophy, I returned back home to Manhasset for the summer. One night, while I was out at a local restaurant, I looked up and saw the most beautiful woman in the world. It was, Liz, my grammar school sweetheart. When I was growing up in Manhasset, I attended St. Mary's Elementary School. I can remember the first day of fourth grade. I was sitting in the back of the classroom with all of the other wise guys and I saw a little blond-haired girl named, Liz. She was the most beautiful girl I had ever seen in my life. It was really love at first sight. I finally got the nerve to ask Liz to be my girlfriend in seventh grade and she said, "Yes." I messed it up in eighth grade. We broke up and I went away to boarding school. We didn't see each other again until I had my injury. Liz came to visit me in the hospital, but several more years went by where we didn't see each other.

When I saw Liz in the restaurant that night, it was like the first day of fourth grade all over again. I couldn't believe how beautiful she was. Liz explained that she was going through a divorce and that she and her two daughters, Lauren and Katy, had moved in with her parents in Oyster Bay, New York. We had made arrangements to get together later that summer so that I could meet her kids.

That July, I met Lauren and Katy at an outdoor festival on Long Island. They were adorable kids, really smart, with great personalities. Liz and I went to the movies one time and to dinner on one other occasion. Over the next few years we had limited contact. Liz's marriage was annulled and she was busy raising her girls and going to school. I was entrenched in the formation program and discerning where God was calling me in my life. Ironically, I could see Liz's family's house in Oyster Bay across the water from the property of the seminary in Huntington. There would be days at the seminary when I'd look across the water at Liz's house and wonder how she and the girls were doing. One year, Liz's family invited me over for Thanksgiving dinner. While we were eating, I could see the bell tower of the seminary through a window in their home, now from the other side of the water.

Frank Bice

Chapter VIII
The Exodus

As I approached my fourth year in the diocesan formation program, I still hadn't resolved the marriage issue. After completing a year of philosophy and two years of theology, each seminarian is required to spend a year in active ministry, called a pastoral year. I was assigned to St. John the Baptist Diocesan High School. This was an awesome assignment and I loved every minute of it. During my pastoral year, I had the opportunity to teach, coach, preach at Mass, and counsel the students. Graciously, the principal allowed me to bring my dog, Jug, with me. It was in the hallways of St. John's that Jug learned to push my chair. This was the good news and the bad news. It was great that Jug could push my chair, but we only traveled where he wanted to go!

When I completed my pastoral year, I knew I had to take leave from the seminary system. I was only eighteen months away from being ordained a transitional deacon, (which is when you make your permanent promises), and two years away from being ordained a priest. At that time, I learned that my old boarding school was looking for a teacher and a coach. When they offered me the position, I said, "Yes."

Back at my old boarding school, Canterbury in New Milford, Connecticut, I had the best job on the planet Earth. I had an apartment on campus, taught theology, and coached football, basketball, and lacrosse. When I became the Head Football Coach, I faced a number of challenges. I was coaching the sport that I was playing when I became paralyzed, and the team had not won a game in four years.

At our first team meeting I explained how I was injured, we set goals for the upcoming season, and we went to work.

Every year Canterbury opened up the season by playing Avon Old Farms, a powerhouse in Connecticut.

The week of the opening game, I drove my van up to Avon, Connecticut, and got permission from a farmer for my team to do our pre-game warm-ups on his farm. The day of the game, we suited up in Avon's locker room, got back on the bus, and performed our warm-ups on the farm. A minute before the opening kick-off, we arrived at the game field. My players sprinted off the bus and stormed the field. My idea was that we would use that momentum to carry us through the game. It worked for the first half. In the second half we got crushed.

We tried everything to break the losing streak. We even had trick plays. We had one play where the offensive line would take their position on the ball, the quarterback would touch the center's back, and then start walking toward our bench. As he approached the bench, he looked like he was going to call a timeout. The quarterback would say, "Wait a minute Coach, this play is never going to work!" As soon as the quarterback said the word "work," the center would snap the ball back to the fullback and he would run the ball up the middle of the field. The play was designed to catch the defense off guard. When we tried the play, the center snapped the ball over the fullback's head and we lost several yards.

We kept losing. I'll never forget the second to last game of the season. We were playing against Westminster at home. It was freezing cold. There was driving rain mixed with hail and sleet. We were getting pounded. At halftime we were losing 42:0. During the break, my players used to carry me down the field house steps for the halftime speech. My players were beaten down, freezing, and exhausted. They looked like they were ready to quit. As they carried me down the field house steps, I can remember thinking, "What am I possibly going to say to these guys to make them want to finish the game?" I said the following to my players that day, "I love you guys and I'm proud of you because you haven't given up. And you know what? There's no way we are going to beat these guys today. We are going to lose, but we are going to lose together. Years ago I put on my helmet, ran onto a football field and never walked off. Some people might say that I lost that day and lost everyday for the rest of my life. I know that my job is to put on my helmet everyday and to go out into life, remain positive, and to do the best I can. If that is considered losing, then I will gladly put on my helmet everyday and go out there and lose. Your job, today and everyday, for the rest of your lives, is to put on your helmets and go out and do the best you can. It's not about the scoreboard today or any day. It's not about winning. It never is. It's about putting on your helmets and going out there knowing you are going to lose. It's not about how you feel. It's about love. It's about real love that never counts the cost. It's about putting on your helmets, knowing that you are going to lose, but doing it for your friends. Today I want you to put on your helmets and go out there and lose together as a team. This is about your commitment to each other and finishing what you started. I promise you this, if you have the courage to finish the game, you will never forget this day for the rest of your lives. In life you are going to lose more often than you are going to win. So put on your helmets, and let's get out there and lose together as a team." We played pretty tough in the second half and we finished the game. Ultimately, we lost the next game, the final contest of the season. Now we had a five-year losing streak.

The next year, we came back out and we were pretty strong. We lost a few close games and then we beat Berkshire at home. The losing streak was finally over. The next game we beat Westminster, the team that had crushed us in the freezing rain the year before. When we beat Westminster, I can remember calling the team together on their field and saying, "Fellas, you just beat the team that killed us last year. This is what happens when you don't give up. Eventually good things happen. You should be proud of yourselves." And then I made the classic mistake. When you are dealing with high school kids especially, you should never tell them what NOT to do. While I still had the team together on the field, I said, "Let's be smart tonight. You can hang out together and have fun, but, no one, I repeat, no one, is to drink any alcohol tonight. Do you understand me?" In unison they replied, "Yes, Coach!"

The next morning I got the call. Seven of my seniors had been caught drinking the night before. I had to take away a captainship and suspend all seven for the next game. We lost that game. The wind was out of our sails and we lost the final game of the season.

I like to tell this story to illustrate the importance of the Sacrament of Reconciliation. In the early Church, there were only two sacraments: Baptism and the Lord's Supper (the ancient version of our modern day Mass). The early Christians believed that Jesus was coming back any day. So they had one Baptism for the forgiveness of sins and then they waited. They waited for Jesus to return. Over time, it started to become clear that Jesus wasn't coming back as soon as they had originally thought. A new challenge arose for the community. How would they handle it when someone sinned? If you only had one Baptism for the forgiveness of sins, what would they do when someone committed a sin after their Baptism? The Sacrament of Reconciliation grew out of the Sacrament of Baptism.

Now, if you or I commit a sin, can we go directly to God, and can God forgive our sin? I believe we can go directly to God. He made us. He is all powerful. I believe we can go directly to God and He can forgive us. That's not the point of the Sacrament of Reconciliation. The Sacrament of Reconciliation is about being reconciled with the community. When you or I throw a rock into a pond, there's always a ripple effect. Whenever we are engaged in any action, whether good or bad, there is always a ripple effect. Our actions always affect other people. Whenever we commit a sin, it's never just about us. It always affects other people too. For the early Christians, it was all about their personal salvation in the context of living in the right relationship with God and the community. Before His Ascension into Heaven, Jesus had commanded His followers to be one, unified, community. The early Christians took that command seriously, and so should we. The early Christians understood that certain standards had to be upheld in order to be in good standing with the community. It's out of respect for the individual and the community. That is why it was necessary for the Sacrament of Reconciliation to grow out of the Sacrament of Baptism. It empowers the individual to be born again, to be given a clean slate, and to exist in the right relationship with God and the community.

Now, were my seven seniors who went out drinking good kids? They were great kids. They just made a mistake. If everyone learned from their mistake, maybe it was a good thing that it happened. But their actions didn't just affect themselves. Their actions affected the entire season. The consequences of their decision hurt the other members of the team. In fairness to the group as a whole, the players had to be suspended to be able to return and be in good standing with the team again. To be part of any organization, certain standards have to be upheld. This is true of the Church as well. The Sacrament of Reconciliation is a free and generous gift that gives us the opportunity to exist in the right relationship with God and each other. In sports, an individual's performance is only valuable in the context of the team. In our faith life, our personal relationship with God can only have real meaning in the context of the community.

The other memorable team I coached at Canterbury was the Boys' Junior Varsity Basketball Team. Sports at this school were mandatory. Every kid had to play a sport every season. If a kid didn't make a junior varsity team, he could play intramurals. One year, I had eighteen kids tryout for J.V. basketball. These were the nicest kids in the world, but not very talented basketball players. So I made another regrettable decision. I decided that I wasn't going to cut anyone. My reasoning was that six players would gladly step down and play intramurals. With intramurals, they would have Wednesdays and weekends off, and they wouldn't have to travel to away games-which were usually halfway across New England! I called all eighteen players over and said, "Fellas, I'm not making any cuts this year, I promise. I need six of you to step down on your own. Let me see a show of hands." Not one hand went up. I said, "Fellas please, I need six of you to step down." No one would quit. True to my word, I kept all eighteen.

When the season started, we would have five players on the floor, and thirteen on the bench. My bench looked like the Russian Army! Invariably, we would be getting crushed. I'd call timeout with five minutes left in the game and we would be losing something like 90:20. During the timeout, I'd say, "If we hold them under 100 points, and we score 25, pizza in my apartment after the game." On occasion, we would hold our opponents to 99 and we would score 25 at the buzzer. My eighteen lunatics would run around the gym like they just won the NBA Championship! The other teams didn't want to make eye contact with us because they thought we were crazy. I can't tell you how much money I spent on pizza that season.

For away games, my players had to carry me on the bus. They would practically kill me getting me on and off the bus. One day, we had an away game. As my players carried me on the bus, snow flurries were beginning to fall. The game was a nightmare. We lost something like 115:14. Meanwhile, the flurries outside turned into a blizzard. After the game as one of my players was wheeling me from the gym to the parking lot, neither one of us noticed where the curb ended and the parking lot began. So as my front wheels went over the curb, I fell out of my chair. As I was lying there with my face in the snow, I was thinking, "It can't get any worse than this." Just then, one of my players came running up to me and yelled, "Coach, I can't fine my shoe!" When I heard these words I thought, "Wow, I'm going to kill you." But then I started laughing because I realized how funny it was.

When you think about it, in sports, it's really not about winning. It's about doing the best you can and being there for your teammates. It's the same thing in life too. All God asks of any of us, is to be faithful. He's not looking for perfect people. He's looking for faithful people. The Bible is full of examples of God choosing to work through imperfect people. In the New Testament, Jesus chose twelve Apostles, many of whom were considered outcasts by society. In the Old Testament, I can't think of a better example than, Moses. When God chose Moses to be the leader of the Israelites, Moses didn't want to do it. Moses said, "Please Lord, choose someone else, I have a speech impediment. I can't do it!" God answered Moses by saying, "Don't worry. I'll send your brother, Aaron, to be your mouthpiece. Just be a good leader, and you will be fine."

So Moses leads the Israelites for forty years through the desert, during the period known as the Exodus. The Exodus will become the defining event for the Israelites and the most important theme throughout the entire Old Testament. Moses gives his whole life over to faithfully serving God and the community. He endures unimaginable hardship and sacrifice. Just as he is about to cross the Jordan River and enter into the Promised Land, Moses dies, and Joshua takes over. The world would see Moses as a failure. He died right before entering the Promised Land! What God is saying to you and to me is that it's not about the destination, it's about the journey. In life, and in sports, it's not about winning. It's about putting on your helmet everyday and remaining faithful, regardless of whether you win or lose. It's about doing the best you can and remaining faithful. It's about living in the right relationship with God and each other.

Frank Bice

Chapter IX
Do You Love Me?

My favorite passage in Scripture has always been the resurrection scene in John's Gospel. Jesus and Peter are on the beach and our Lord asks him three times, "Do you love me? Peter is hurt because Jesus asked him three times. It brings to mind how Peter had denied Jesus three times during His persecution.

While I was teaching and coaching at my old boarding school, Liz and I began dating. Before long, we got engaged. I felt like the luckiest person on the planet Earth. I was going to marry the love of my life, my best friend, my soul mate, and the most beautiful woman in the world. I was also going to become the step-father of the greatest kids in the world, Lauren and Katy. I felt like I died and went to heaven. Then I felt like I just died. Everything fell apart.

When we got engaged, Liz had finished school, was working on Wall Street, and doing a great job of raising her girls on Long Island. I was teaching six days a week and coaching three sports. Neither one of us had time to breathe. We made an effort to see each other every chance we could, but in time it became clear that our lifestyles were completely incompatible. On the saddest day of my life, we broke off the engagement. My life went from being full of love and excitement, to lonely and dreary.

Life at the boarding school continued to be good, but without Liz in my life, it wasn't the same. I was convinced that Liz would meet someone else on Wall Street, get married, and that she and the girls would live happily ever after without me. Years went by, and we had no communication.

While I was teaching, I was invited to attend a birthday party on Long Island for one of the young priests, who, years before, had asked me to consider the priesthood. While I was at the party, I bumped into Bishop McGann. Bishop McGann said to me, "Frank, I heard you and Liz called off the wedding. Maybe your vocation really is to become a priest. I'd like you to come back to the seminary."

I loved Bishop McGann. As I drove back to Connecticut that night, I was flattered that he wanted me to consider the priesthood again, but, I was still torn about where God was calling me. I prayed about it and said, "Yes."

The following year, I found myself back in the seminary. My dog, Jug, was still with me. Once again, I was treated with the utmost respect and encouragement. My new seminarian classmates were incredibly generous with their friendship and support. Now, I was fifteen months away from my permanent promises, and I was sweating bullets. I loved the Church, my faith was strong, and the formation program continued to be excellent. The classes were outstanding. I prayed the Rosary every day. I also developed a devotion to St. Therese of Lisieax, known as the Little Flower. I found out about a shrine devoted to the Little Flower out in Hauppauge, Long Island.

Every morning I prayed the Rosary with a group of seminarians. After classes, I drove out to the Shrine of the Little Flower and I prayed about my vocation harder than I had ever prayed in my life. When I was one week away from becoming ordained a transitional deacon and making my permanent promises that would never allow me to marry, I was out at the shrine in the pouring rain begging God for mercy. I pleaded, "Please Lord, I'll do whatever you want me to do, just give me peace about the decision." Just as I prayed that prayer, I heard a voice deep in my heart say, "Go home!" So I listened. I got in my van and drove immediately to my mother's house in Manhasset. As I pulled my van in the driveway in the pouring rain, I looked in my rearview mirror and saw Liz. We had absolutely no communication for five years. Liz was driving her daughter, Lauren, to a basketball game at St. Mary's and they pulled up behind me. When they saw my van, Lauren insisted they follow me in the driveway. We got out of our cars in the pouring rain and hugged each other. I realized at that moment how much I still loved Liz. Miraculously, she was still single.

Your Cross is Your Gift

The next day I drove out to the Shrine of Our Lady of the Island in Manorville and I prayed. I came to the conclusion that Liz and I should get married. That day I met with Bishop McGann and I resigned from the formation program. Graciously, he gave me his blessing, hugged me, and said, "God bless you Frank, I hope you are happy no matter what you decide." Now I was free to marry Liz.

There was only one problem. Liz didn't want to have anything to do with me. After we had called off our engagement five years earlier, Liz didn't want to get hurt again. It was a nightmare. For months I called and tried to see Liz and the girls, but Liz kept a safe distance. When I reached the point of absolute desperation, I surrendered. In my prayer I said, "Lord, whatever is best for Liz and the girls, let that happen. If it's better for them to live their lives without me, please don't let us get back together. Whatever Your will is, I accept it." Almost immediately, when I prayed that prayer, Liz came around. At the beach on the Fourth of July, I asked Liz to marry me. She said, "Yes!"

Four months later in November we were married. It was the happiest day of my life. Liz was the most beautiful bride in the world. Lauren and Katy served in the wedding. We had twelve priests concelebrating at the ceremony, many of whom had been my classmates in the seminary. Jug ran down the center aisle of the church at the end of the Mass.

Chapter X
The Resurrection

Through the years, married life has been Heaven on Earth. Liz is the greatest wife in the world. Before we got married, I didn't know Liz was such a great cook. Liz surprises me everyday with all of her love and amazing talents. Lauren and Katy are awesome step-daughters. They are beautiful and great in every possible way.

After a very successful career on Wall Street, Liz decided to pursue her true passion, teaching! Liz graduated from Columbia Teacher's College, taught for many years where it all began at St. Mary's in Manhasset, and is presently completing her PhD in Literacy for At-Risk Learners.

When they were in high school, both Lauren and Katy attended St. Anthony's in Huntington, Long Island. While they were students there, my good friend from the seminary, Father Brian Barr was the school chaplain. Anytime the girls needed anything at school, I'd call Father Brian and he would take care of it.

After a wonderful life, my dog, Jug, had to be put down because he had become riddled with cancer. That morning, Lauren and Katy had missed the bus to school. On the way to the veterinarian's office, I dropped off the girls at St. Anthony's with Jug in the van. Father Brian came out to the van and gave Jug his final blessing.

Father Brian Barr is currently Director of Vocations for the Diocese of Rockville Center. He still loves playing Irish music on the banjo.

Jimmy "Bone Breaker" Scacalossi, left the seminary after our pastoral year. He is happily married, has three beautiful children, and is head of the Theology Department at Regis High School in New York City.

Of my roommates from the hospital, Jacob became a successful lawyer. Seamus is happily married and has a great job. The last I heard of Mike, I saw him being interviewed on a television news program. He was arguing for the legalization of marijuana because it could help people with disabilities control their "muscle spasms."

A few years ago, after spending twenty-five years in bed, my friend Vinny passed away. When I attended the funeral, those adopted boys, now men, were the pallbearers. As they guided their father's body down the aisle of the church, I'll never forget the look of strength, courage, conviction, and determination in the eyes of those men and I thought, "What a gift!" What a gift Ann and Vinny were to these men. What a gift these men will be to the world. These men, like their parents, will be Witnesses of Hope.

My roommate from Siena, Rence, has led an amazing life. Rence and Virginia got married and have six of the most beautiful kids you've ever seen in your life. Rence is currently an account executive at Comedy Central.

The modern day parable of the Mustard Seed was about Dave Pietramala. He is presently the Head Lacrosse Coach at Johns Hopkins. He was won two National Championships as their Head Coach and has been named Coach of the Year in Division I Lacrosse. Dave is considered the greatest defenseman in the history of lacrosse.

Over the years since I left the school, the Canterbury football program won several New England Championships. In my heart, the greatest team was the one that had the courage to finish the game, when we were getting crushed in the freezing rain.

Several years later, the Miller brothers still take turns helping me get dressed and into my wheelchair in the mornings. Occasionally we go for a swim!

My step-daughters are all grown up now. Lauren is completing her PhD in Psychology and is engaged to an outstanding young man. Katy graduated from college with honors, is working in an advocacy office, and studying broadcast journalism in graduate school.

Years after Liz and I got married, I entered the Permanent Diaconate Formation program. A permanent deacon can be married and serve the Church in that capacity. I believed God was calling me to put to good use all of my training in the seminary. Three years later, I was ordained a permanent deacon. The morning of my ordination, I read in Scripture, "He predestined us to be His adopted sons." When the bishop laid his hands on my head, I felt the Holy Spirit enter my body like a burst of wind. At that moment, I knew that I had been adopted.

Over the years, Liz and I have started doing parishes missions together. The feedback from our missions has been very positive. The only criticism we've received is that they would like to hear more from Liz and less from me!

In the fall of 2007, Liz and I were asked to give a mission at Holy Cross Church in Rochester, NY. While we were in Rochester, I gave a talk to the football team at St. John Fisher College, where I had my injury twenty-seven years earlier. After I spoke to the team in their new stadium, I found myself on the exact spot on the old field where I broke my neck twenty-seven years earlier. It was a beautiful sunny day. As I looked down at the grass, I started to pray, "Thank You, Jesus," over and over again. I then had a conversation with myself, envisioning the injured twenty-one year old football player lying there in his football equipment. I told him, "I love you so much and I'm proud of you. Thank you for giving all that you had and for leaving it all on the field. I love you and I couldn't be any more proud of you!" And then the twenty-one year old football player looked up at me and said, "Thank you for not giving up and for going ahead with your life. Thank you for making all of my dreams come true. Thank you for marrying my childhood sweetheart, Liz. Thank you for becoming a deacon. Thank you for becoming a coach. I will love you and be there for you the rest of your life." Just as he said this, I looked up and saw the most beautiful woman in the world walking toward me, my wife, Liz.

Your Cross is Your Gift

Frank Bice